An Escape from Communist Vietnam:

A True Story of Love, Courage and Struggles

Written by

Ann Tran-Mace

Edited by

Mark Trevor

Copyright @ 2015 by Ann Tran-Mace

All rights reserved. No part of this book may be reproduced, transmitted, or stored in an information retrieval system in any form or by any means, graphic, electronic, or mechanical, including photocopying, taping, and recording, without prior written permission of the publisher.

ISBN-13: 978-1517765699

ISBN-10: 1517765692

Dedication

This book is about you, mother. You are my definition of sacrifice and unselfishness. I will always love and treasure you.

This book is for you, Matt and Lila, my precious children. It is my hope that this documentation of my family's experiences will help you learn to appreciate what you have and not take anything or anyone for granted. I love you too much not to share these experiences with you.

For our loving God, may this story be a testimony for me and others that you are alive and dwell in us.

Acknowledgements

In memory of my father, Tien Tran, and my great uncle, Tran Van Khac, whose wisdom and extraordinary execution made it possible for my family to find hope.

To my mother, Ngai Doan, and my siblings, Anh Thong, Chi Dung, Anh Minh, Anh Thai and Man: Thank you for giving your time to share your amazing stories with me. Without your accounts of past events, this book would not have been possible.

To my husband, Rick, and my in-laws, Charlene, Kathryn and Fred: Thank you for your love, kindness and continuous support. We are blessed to have you in our lives.

To my good and honest friend, Mark, who had helped me with this book from start to finish: I cannot thank you enough for your encouragement and countless efforts in editing my story.

To all American men and women who have served to protect our freedom, including those during the Vietnam War who fought to prevent the spread of communism: We will always be grateful for your support.

Table of Contents

Preface		1
Introduction		3
Chapter 1	My Parents' Early Years	7
Chapter 2	My Father and the Vietnamese "Cinderella"	11
Chapter 3	The Wedding and Marriage	19
Chapter 4	Viet Cong Take Control	41
Chapter 5	The Escape	51
Chapter 6	On the Pacific Ocean	59
Chapter 7	Malaysia and Pulau Bidong Island	69
Chapter 8	Challenges in America	85
Reflection		99
Family Trees		105
Map of Vietnam		108
Glossary		109

Preface

October 1978

"Wake-up, wake-up, Be Anh," my sweet sister (Chi Dung) whispered. I woke up wondering where we were. It was very dark and we seemed to be in an enclosed area on a boat. At the age of seven, I was afraid and confused. Earlier, around 5:30 p.m., we were having dinner at a restaurant. I must have fallen asleep after dinner. I could not see anything but found out later that we were on an old wooden boat about 40 feet long and 10 feet wide. The cabin was about six by six feet. There was a cover over a hole that was two by two feet. That hole dropped into an area about four feet high, eight feet wide and thirty feet long. We were hiding in that bottom area of the boat and were not the only ones down there. I didn't know what was going on when my sister woke me up. "Shhh. We are on our way to America…the land of the free with great opportunities for our family," she said excitedly. I felt a sense relief and was less fearful, but I thought, "How did we get here? What happened to our three-story home? Did it burn down?"

Introduction

Writing this story took me through an emotional roller coaster ride. I found myself crying to sleep all over again. I had to take breaks in between writing to let my emotions recover.

Vietnam was a country that seemed to be a constant war zone. School, work and all aspects of life were perpetually being interrupted and/or lost. Just when you thought you had built a successful business in order to give your family a quality life, it was disrupted or taken away. Months or years of hard work could be gone in an instant, and you would find yourself rebuilding your life all over again.

We wondered when Vietnam would finally have peace, stability and economic prosperity. But with the Viet Cong (Vietnamese Communists) in control, it was nearly impossible to see the light at the end of the tunnel.

This book is the true story about my family's experiences before, during and after the Vietnam

War, which ended in 1975. The story highlights our faithful escape to the blessed land of America.

I share this story to encourage others, especially my two children, to continue to strive no matter how hard life seems. Despite our flaws and obstacles, God will deliver us through the most difficult times.

Even today, I remember my parents praying throughout our entire escape process. It was difficult not to believe that God was with us all the way.

Our initial goal was to arrive (by boat) at a refugee camp in Singapore, but there were many risks and obstacles ahead of us.

Considering the risks, most would not have made any attempts to leave the country. My parents had the option to leave Vietnam in 1975 (after the Viet Cong took over), but they decided to stay. They soon regretted that decision and planned their escape in 1978.

Had my parents left in 1975, I would not have lost three crucial years of school (Kindergarten through second grade). Thus, starting third grade in America without any formal education and without a word of English seemed impossible for me considering my imperfections and obstacles.

My aunt (Co Nam) and her husband (Chu Mai) left Vietnam right after the war ended in 1975. They had the luxury of a flight directly to America. Unfortunately for us, my parents had decided to stay. Perhaps this was part of God's plan. Having survived such a life-changing experience proved to me that our God was alive in us.

What was the primary motivation for our escape? I had always wondered. Later in this story, you will discover the main reason we had to flee from the Viet Cong.

Chapter 1

My Parents' Early Years

In 1944, Vietnam was once again in a war zone. My grandparents had to abandon their home and their hard-earned, hand-made embroidery business in Saigon (Ho Chi Minh City). They moved to the district of Thu Duc to avoid increased danger. Their oldest son, Bac Chinh, was in service for the Vietnamese government. At this time, my mother (Ngai Doan) was nine years old and had six siblings--one of which was a newborn. Milk and many staples were scarce due to the war, and a quarter gallon of milk per week was not enough for her newborn brother, Cau Toan. Therefore, my grandparents hand-mashed boiled potatoes, extended cooking of rice soup, and did whatever was necessary to keep their newborn baby from starving to death.

Through my grandfather's connections, my mother and her older sister, Bac Nguyet, were allowed inside the Japanese compound to sell goods. My mother was able to sell three baskets of goods per day inside the compound. The goods ranged from steamed sweet potatoes to cookies to candies. She could only carry one basket at a time. After her basket was emptied, she went to the market to get it refilled. After the second refill (third basket) was emptied, it was night time, and she headed home for bed. My mother's sales of goods at the compound were her family's only source of income during 1944-1946. It might seem to be child labor to most Americans, but to my mother, it was love. She, perhaps more than anyone else in the family, was helping her family survive.

The Japanese were remarkably generous to a nine-year-old girl trying to keep her family alive. When they paid her for the goods, they told her that she could have the rest. They patted her on the head and said, "Keep the change, cute little girl…" She was their in-house snack bar. Instead of going to the market to get the snacks, they bought them from my mother.

There were large pots of food cooked inside the compound, so they told Ngai to bring her older sibling, Bac Nguyet, and as many food containers as possible in order to carry home the food. It took the two sisters a couple of trips to bring home all the food. This extra food from the compound was enough to feed the whole family of nine (two parents and seven children). Furthermore, some of the money my mother earned was kept as savings for the family.

After 1946, the war ended and they moved back to Saigon. Their home and business were lost during the war, so my grandparents (on my mother's side) had to rent a house and rebuild their hand-made embroidery business. This was when my mother met my father. They were neighbors.

Due to a medical condition, my grandfather (Tran Van Nhan) passed away two months before my father, Tien, was born. Therefore, Tien came into this world in 1935, without a father. His uncle, known as Tran Van Khac, and his wife asked my grandmother (Tu Thi Ky) to let them take my father as their son, but my grandmother declined the offer. Plus, my great grandmother was available to help her raise my father. It would have been very difficult for my grandmother to give up her newborn unless the situation was absolutely unavoidable. My grandmother and great grandmother did their best to raise my father.

In 1939, my grandmother remarried and my great uncle again asked for my father to come live with him. Traditionally, if the mother remarried, the child would need to move out. But my father refused to go with his uncle. At the age of four, he was very attached to his mother and grandmother, so it would have been very difficult for anyone to take him from them. As a result, my father ended up moving in with his grandmother.

In 1945, my great uncle and his wife asked my grandmother and great grandmother for the third time to let them take my father as their son. They had three daughters and had always wanted to have a son. My great uncle was the founder of the Vietnamese Scouting Association and the first Vietnamese to make and sell ice cream in Vietnam. He also owned commercial and residential properties in Saigon and Da Lat. Tran Van Khac was an honest, hardworking and successful businessman. My grandmother realized that my father would be in good hands, so she accepted their third offer. My father came to live with my great uncle as his son. At the age of ten, Tien Tran officially had a father and an opportunity to attend school!

Chapter 2

My Father and the Vietnamese "Cinderella"

After my mother's family moved back to Saigon in 1946, the two families became good friends. Like Cinderella, my mother worked from dawn to dusk. She continued to help her parents run the handmade embroidery business, as well as cook, babysit her younger siblings, and do household chores while her other siblings were in school. I have asked myself many times, why did they have my mother do all of this and not her siblings? It was because she was willing, reliable, quick and efficient. At this point, she had another newborn sibling, Co Nhan, to care for. (There were now a total of seven siblings.) My great uncle's daughters (Bac Thu and Bac Phuong) often asked to have some playtime with my mother, but she could only come out to play after 8 p.m. when most of her work was done.

When my mother, Ngai, came over to play with my great uncle's daughters, Bac Thu and Bac Phuong (technically, my father's cousins), she met my father, Tien. I don't know if it was love-at-first-sight, but my father had heard many positive comments about my mother. My grandparents claimed my mother to be their right-hand daughter. She was helpful, swift, and dependable. According to my grandparents, she sacrificed the most for her family.

Ngai and Tien became good friends. My mother did not have much playtime with my father and his sisters (technically his cousins) due to her huge workload. Nevertheless, she tried to come over after her work to spend time with them.

In 1951, Tien and his family moved to Da Lat, which is a gorgeous city in Vietnam with nice, cool temperatures all year-round. Tran Van Khac opened his second ice cream shop (Viet Hung on Thanh Thai street) on a hill overlooking the beautiful city. It was one of the most-visited ice cream shops in Da Lat. Due to the pleasant, spring-like weather all year-round, Da Lat was one of the most popular cities in Vietnam.

My father – Da Lat, Vietnam waterfalls

Da Lat, Vietnam waterfalls

A few weeks after my father moved to Da Lat, he (then aged 16) sent letters to my mother, addressed to her older brother, Bac Chinh. Culturally, dating or having a boyfriend/girlfriend was not allowed in Vietnam. Bac Chinh gave the letters to my mother. My father had asked my mother to wait for him--not to marry anyone else. He indicated that he would be in Saigon once a month for his uncle's business and would then visit her and her siblings.

Just as he had promised, my father visited them once a month. As part of the Vietnamese culture, she was not allowed to go out alone with him. So for their date all of her siblings, with the exception of the two youngest, went along with them. At the time, seven siblings were old enough to join them, and they all wanted to go. Those were some expensive dates. It was a good thing he could visit Saigon only once a month!

In 1954, the Viet Cong defeated the French colonial administration in Vietnam and took over Hanoi, which became the capital of North Vietnam. By that time, the hand-made embroidery business did not do as well. My mother (aged 19) went to trade school and completed third place out of over five thousand students. She was in the top one percent and was offered a teaching job at that trade school but declined to start her own business. She became one of the best seamstresses in town, designing and custom-making Ao Dai, which is Vietnam's most popular dress. Every dress had to be measured and custom-made for each customer. It was created to perfectly fit each person's unique figure. My mother was able to flawlessly custom-make these dresses for her customers. She earned about seven times the teaching salary offered to her at the trade school.

Ao Dai is Vietnam's most popular dress

My mother's business thrived, and she continued to help her parents pay their bills. As usual, she worked from dawn to dusk so her siblings could have the opportunity to attend school. My father continued to visit her in the evening each month, followed by an expensive date with more of her siblings joining the crowd. My father probably came back to Da Lat with an empty wallet after each visit to Saigon.

One evening in 1953, my father took my mother and her eight siblings to a Hoi Cho (fall festival) at the Saigon So Thu (Saigon Botanical and Zoological Garden). In this zoological garden, there was a bridge that crossed the Thi Nghe channel. Due to the fall festival activities, there were many light displays and beautiful scenes to observed from this bridge, so everyone wanted to get on it to get a good view and take some pictures.

As the bridge was filling up with people, my mother's younger siblings also wanted to get on, and they did. Within minutes, people were yelling, "Please back out! Please get off of the bridge! People are dying here!" My father took this opportunity to grab my mother's hand and said, "Let's get your siblings out now. We should get off of this bridge. It is not worth it." People were still coming in as they both got her siblings off.

Due to the commotion, my mother did not notice that my father had taken hold of her hand. Once out, she realized he was holding her hand. As he was the first man to hold her hand, sweat was exuding through the pores of her skin. She had to pull away at times to wipe the moisture from her hands. It was a romantic but embarrassing moment for my mother.

The next morning, that famous bridge was in the headlines of the newspaper. Unfortunately, over twenty people had died that night. Most were crushed and trampled, and a few had fallen off the bridge and drowned. If my parents and her siblings had gotten on the bridge just thirty minutes earlier, they probably would have been victims as well.

While my mother was busy in Saigon, my father had his first exposure to Christianity in Da Lat, where there were missionaries from the U.S. and the Philippines who had come to spread the word of God. They organized a non-profit Baptist organization known as Hoi Hoan Cau Hai Tuong cua Tin Lanh. Within this organization, English was also taught. My father was mainly interested in learning English, but little did he know he was learning something much more important--the Bible. He then accepted Jesus Christ as his Lord and Savior and became close friends with a Philippine missionary couple. They spoke English fluently but needed to learn Vietnamese in order to better spread the Gospel. My father helped them learn Vietnamese as they taught him English. This marked the beginning of his new life with a fresh perspective.

My father (1954)

Chapter 3

The Wedding and Marriage

Ngai (1955)

Tien (1955)

A year later, when both of my parents were twenty, my great uncle thought it was a good time for them to get married, so he told my grandfather, "I think it is time for Ngai and Tien to get married. They are old enough." My grandfather and grandmother replied, "I think we should give Ngai a couple more years. She just started her tailor business at home. She hired a few ladies to help and things are going well so far. Maybe we should ask her to get her opinion about marriage right now." My grandparents were right--my mother was not ready to get married yet. She wanted to focus on the business and help her family. By this time, my mother had a total of eleven siblings! (I am not sure how my mother managed to help my grandmother with all those siblings. My sister, Chi Dung, once told me that our grandmother was slightly odd. I can see why. If I had 12 children to care for, I would go crazy as well!)

Four years later, in 1959, at the age of twenty-four, my father asked for my mother's hand in marriage. As part of our culture, one was not allowed to marry unless the parents or guardians on both sides approved of the marriage. In this case, both approved, but my grandparents asked for my mother to stay home one more year. After all, she was their right-hand daughter and it would be a big adjustment for her family without her help. My great uncle declined the request, stating that my mother and father were old enough (both aged 24) to get married. He said to my grandfather, "It is about time she moved on to start her own life. Do you want her to be an old maiden? She deserves a good marriage. If ever needed, I can provide for them and their five or six future children. You have nothing to worry about." I believed my great uncle wanted to free my mother from the long, tedious labor she had been enduring for the past fourteen years. But for my mother, it was all well worth it. She lived to serve others and that in itself brought her much happiness. Regardless, she had to move on to start her new life.

Traditionally, the wedding was hosted at the bride's house. The groom's side of the family would bring gifts for the bride's family. Each person from the groom's side of the family would hold a gift that was wrapped in clear, red gift-wrap paper. The gifts ranged from whole grilled pig to fruits to cakes.

Whole grilled pig

Gifts from groom's family ranging from teas to cakes to fruits

After the two families greeted one another, the bride would emerge from her room and greet everyone. The bride and groom then exchanged vows.

As my mother was coming out from her room to greet the groom and his family, her two youngest brothers, Cau Bich (aged 6) and Cau Hai (aged 3), pulled her back crying, "Chi Ngai, please don't get married. Please stay with us." They turned to my father yelling, "Anh Tien, please don't take Chi Ngai from us." They were crying as if their own mother was leaving them. The two boys--kicking, screaming and crying--were finally pulled away from my mother and taken into a room upstairs. Everyone thought it was hilarious, but it must have been an emotionally powerful moment for my mother. Unlike the fairy tale Cinderella, my mother's family treated her with love and appreciation. They would miss her greatly but knew she would be visiting them soon.

    As part of our culture, the groom and/or his side of the family were responsible for the wedding reception. My great uncle, Tran Van Khac, funded their beautiful wedding reception in Da Lat. In Saigon, my grandparents also gave them a graceful reception. For these occasions, my mother custom-made five of her own wedding dresses, two for the reception in Saigon and three for the one in Da Lat.

My parents' wedding (September 25, 1959)

My grandfather and my great uncle at my parent's wedding reception (1959)

My father handed her one of the wedding bouquets

In Vietnam, the majority of the population was poor, so most Vietnamese did not have a vehicle or their own home. (It is still true today.) The most common methods of transportation were bicycles, motorcycles/mopeds and cyclo (Xich Lo) to name a few. In a cyclo, you are seated on a small carriage as the driver paddles behind you.

Xich Lo (cyclo)

My parents enjoyed riding on the Xich Lo at night to their date destinations. After marriage, they often rode on the Xich Lo for late (after 10 p.m.) dinners and ice creams.

After they were married, my mother drove through the heavily-congested roads in Vietnam. In fact, she was one of the few female drivers, as most women rode bikes. For three years--and with a manual transmission!--she maneuvered through the roads which overflowed with bikes, motorcycles and cyclos.

Needless to say, it was incredibly difficult to get around with a motorcar. (In Vietnam, only the wealthy can afford a vehicle, and an automatic transmission was not available.) Avoiding an accident was almost impossible, so my father decided to keep her from driving. This marked the end of her driving career.

Who could possibly drive in this traffic?

Due to the incredibly dangerous traffic conditions in Vietnam, my mother almost lost one of her brothers, Cau Toan, when he was 9 years old. In 1953, just one year before the Viet Cong defeated the French colonial administration, my uncle (Cau Toan) and a friend were looking at some fish inside a sewage hole at a street corner when a French army jeep struck them.

His friend was run over and died instantly. Cau Toan was thrown 10 feet. He landed on his back, and his head hit the pavement, shattering a back section of his skull. He was unconscious and taken to the hospital. The doctor said his head injury was fatal. "I am sorry. There is not much we can do to help him."

Two days later, he was pronounced dead and taken to the morgue. My grandparents, my mother, and her siblings were devastated. The funeral was to take place in five days, so that evening my mother started to custom-make two funeral gowns for her brother.

The very next day, a morgue employee was performing his normal routine when he heard someone singing a Vietnamese nursery song, "1, 2, 3, the candy man is here..." The employee thought, "A kid must have gotten in the morgue. I need to find him." The song stopped so he could not locate the source of the singing. "That kid must have gotten out," he figured. Ten minutes later, the singing started again. This time, the employee was determined to find the source. He walked through the section where the adults' bodies were kept, then to the children's section where he saw a movement under my uncle's white sheet. My uncle was still singing as the man lifted the sheet. Cau Toan's eyes remained closed as he continued to sing.

Because he was unconscious, no one knew when his heart had started beating again. Cau Toan was moved to a hospital room for intensive care. He remained in a coma for 13 days. After he regained consciousness, his memory was very short, and he would ask the same questions over and over again. He remained in therapy for months before his physical and mental abilities were sufficient enough for him to come home. Astonishingly, they did not perform any surgery on him. A soft spot can still be seen on the back of his head today.

As for marriages in Vietnam, it was very common for the wife to live with her husband's family after marriage since most couples could not afford to have their own place. Yes, as a bride, you were marrying your husband's family as well. It could be stressful enough to live and deal with a husband--let alone having to put up with his whole family. Most likely, your mother-in-law and/or father-in-law would be in charge of your finances and various other things. Thus, marriage was the start of a miserable life for most women in Vietnam.

Although my mother's marriage to my father may seem like a typical marriage for most Americans, it was viewed as a "Cinderella" marriage in Vietnam. (The fairy tale movie had been introduced by the French and was still very popular at the time.)

After the wedding, my mother moved to Da Lat with my father. Not only did my mother not have to live with her in-laws, my parents had an automobile and lived in a home with a business (tire shop) attached, which meant they were well-off compared to most. My father managed a tire shop which was owned by a French company. He also owned a taxi and employed a driver, which allowed my father to bring home some extra money on the side. The driver would receive one-third of the taxi fare as his commission pay and my parents would take two-thirds. All transactions were made in cash, so my parents would have to trust the driver they hired.

My great uncle had always taught my father to be independent. With my great uncle's connections and my father's wisdom, my parents' marriage was the start of an adventurous journey.

My mother noticed there were commercial spaces available nearby their shop, so she asked my great uncle's approval to open a tailor shop. As part of our culture, you have to get approval from the "wise parent" before you could make a business move. Tran Van Khac firmly said, "You have been here for only two months and you want to fly high?" My mother was stunned by his comment. She gently replied, "No, Sir. I just do not want to lose my trait." He said, "You do not need to have your own business. You can help your husband manage the tire shop. If ever needed, I can provide for you both and your future children. You need not to labor from dawn to dusk anymore." My great uncle and his wife wanted my mother to have a relatively labor-free marriage.

Although she married into a wealthy family, she did not experience the freedom she once had with her parents, the freedom to choose her career path. She felt restricted and was very uncomfortable having to depend solely on her husband's income.

Even so, she was blessed to have a smart, loving, reliable husband and very supportive in-laws. Let me provide another example: My great uncle and his wife (Ba Khac) had lost their oldest daughter, Bac Kinh. Due to complications, Bac Kinh passed away after she gave birth to her fourth child. Therefore, they made sure my mother's delivery and postpartum went as pleasant as possible. When my mother was ready to deliver my oldest brother (Anh Thong), Ba Khac booked the largest private postpartum room--with full service--for my mother to stay for two weeks. In fact, all six of us were delivered and stayed two weeks in a large postpartum room. My mother had nursed all of us right after birth. All six of us were fed with the best, most nutritious food a mother could offer!

After my mother gave birth to her first child, my great uncle asked her to get some help, "You need to hire a nanny to help you care for your newborn. You cannot work in that tire shop and care for your newborn at the same time. If you cannot afford a nanny, I will provide you with one."

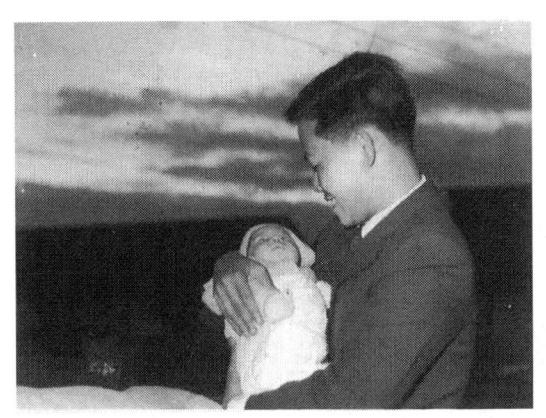

My father holding my oldest brother, Anh Thong (1960)

My parents were blessed with a happy and productive marriage. Impressively, they did not once ask for (or borrow) money from my great uncle. They were able to earn enough to provide for their family without any financial assistance.

During the years of their marriage, my parents often went to many scenic places in Vietnam. My older siblings enjoyed the childhood I never knew existed…

My oldest brother, Anh Thong and sister, Chi Dung in Da Lat (1964)

My brother, Anh Minh and my mother at a farmland in Que, countryside of Vietnam (1964)

My aunt, Co Nam, my mother, uncle, Cau Bich, and my older siblings, Chi Dung, Anh Thong and Anh Minh at Toa Thanh (temple) in Tay Ninh, Vietnam (1965)

My aunt, Co Nam, my uncle, Cau Bich, my mother and older siblings, Anh Thong, Chi Dung and Anh Minh (1966)

My older siblings and mother in Vung Tau, Vietnam (1967)

In 1967, my parents bought a business-front house in Long An for about 240,000 dong, which was equivalent to $156,000 at the time. We had a live-in nanny, a live-in cook and an employee to help operate the retail business. My mother made and sold many wooden clogs. Before making the wooden clogs, each customer had the option to pick the top section of the shoe. Then, my mother would carefully measure and cut each top section to fit the upper part of the customer's feet. Lastly, she cautiously nailed it onto the sides.
(Vietnamese wooden clogs were very popular and beautiful but not so comfortable to stand on for an extended period of time.) She mainly sold wooden clogs but also had other items for sale, everything from snacks to cosmetics. Instead of going to Saigon to purchase these items, most Vietnamese in Long An would buy them from this retail shop.

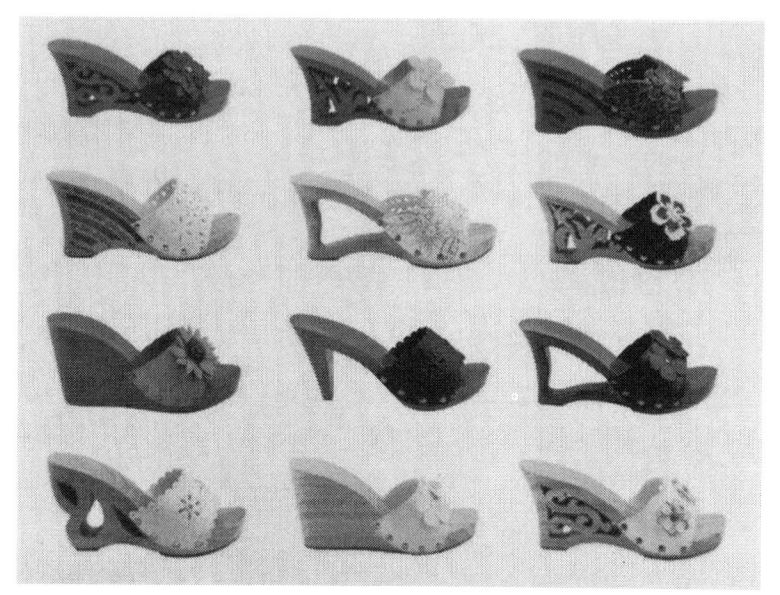

Traditional Vietnamese wooden clogs

In 1971, only four years later, they sold their retail store for about 2.2 million dong--which was a nine hundred percent profit--and moved to Saigon. There in Saigon, they built a three-story business-front house for 4.2 million dong which included an electronic repair shop with books to rent. I thought that was a strange combination but the business continued until our escape.

My parents moved to Saigon after their
5th child, Be Anh, was born (1971)

Saigon Botanical and Zoological Garden (1972)

Chapter 4

Viet Cong Take Control

In 1975, when the North Vietnamese Communists aggressively moved southward, my mother lost one of her brothers, Cau Buu. Along with other doctors, Cau Buu (only 27 years old) was based in Pleiku to service the wounded South Vietnamese soldiers. But he and his four colleagues had to leave the injured soldiers, and join thousands of soldiers and citizens who were fleeing from the charging North Vietnamese army, which was shooting at the crowd! Their mission was to arrive at the Pleiku Air Base to be flown to safety. Due to the panic, the five doctors were separated while crossing a river. But once across, they regrouped-- with the exception of Cau Buu. They searched and called out, but could not find him. He was a good friend and colleague so they did not want to give up the search, but thousands were literally running for their lives so they had to move forward or risk being shot or trampled. My uncle was never seen again.

After Cau Buu's four friends shared their story, my mother prayed and asked God to reveal her brother's whereabouts. That same night, she saw him in her dreams. He knocked on her front door. She opened the door, very happy and relieved to see him, "Buu, you are back!" He replied, "Yes." But his tone was not happy, and he said nothing else. He sadly entered, walking with a cane and favoring his left side. My mother then woke up, believing that God had shown her how he died. She believed he was critically injured on his left side.

(Obviously, I never had the chance to meet Cau Buu, but from what I have gathered, he was a quiet and subtle uncle. He was definitely not the most handsome of the group but always excelled academically.)

Saigon fell and the Viet Cong took control of Vietnam. My aunt (Co Nam) and her husband (Chu Mai), came over to convince my parents to leave with them. My uncle (Chu Mai) and his family were exposed to the Viet Cong when they took over Hanoi in 1954. He said to my parents, "I have seen their ways. I would rather die than to live among the Viet Cong." But my parents had invested 4.2 million dong in the three-story, business-front house and it was doing well. It was not easy for them to give up everything they had built and just leave. Moreover, my great uncle (Tran Van Khac) did not want to leave the country since his wife had passed away shortly before the Viet Cong took control. My parents decided to stay--and prayed for peace. They thought, "Maybe Vietnam will not have any more wars and the Viet Cong will not harm us…." My parents were not exposed to the Viet Cong and did not know their ways. But it took my parents only a few months to see the true picture.

After the Viet Cong took over, they targeted the wealthy and many others. Countless scholars, pastors, educated citizens and successful businessmen were framed, prosecuted and/or executed. A multitude of others were put in concentration camps (known as Re-Education camps). They named the camps as such to hide the horrors inside them. Several families were also forced to move to inhospitable lands called New Economic Zones, or to the outskirts of large cities. Anyone with the slightest threat to communism was to be removed.

So, what was left after they drove away, imprisoned, or murdered their talented and educated citizens? Vietnam was left with a harsh Communist government trying to run Vietnam into an eternal darkness. My family was happy and thriving--until the Viet Cong assumed control of Vietnam. They brought a strong, centrally planned and oppressive government to Vietnam where most citizens suffered for many years.

My parents had to let our nanny and cook go back home. My mother sadly said to them, "I am sorry I cannot keep you, as the Viet Cong will come after us if they think we are well off." They were in tears, begging my mother, "You have been kind to us. You always let us go during the holidays to visit our family. Please keep us; we also need the money to send to our poor family living in Que." (Que was a poverty-stricken, rural area of Vietnam.) My mother painfully replied, "It is very risky. We are not sure what the Viet Cong will do to us. I am so sorry…if things change, I will let you know."

In terms of wages and living standards, there was a large gap between the urban citizens and the rural citizens. (I believe the condition is still true today.) Those in the urban areas had much higher living standards than those dwelling in the rural areas of Vietnam. Vietnamese in the cities, like my parents, were able to hire help (e.g., live-in nannies and live-in cooks) from the rural areas at an affordable amount. Our nanny and cook desperately needed their jobs in order to send money back to their families in the rural areas. It worked out well for everyone--until the Viet Cong came in. They would target and harm those who could afford such services.

My parents had lived through hardships but always had their freedom. For the very first time, they experienced a complete loss of autonomy. They felt as if they were walking on pins and needles--and kept a low profile. After the Viet Cong assumed control, they spared our family but immediately took my great uncle's residential and commercial properties. They sent him and his two daughters to a concentration camp (re-education camp) for a couple of years. What were the charges? According to the Viet Cong, "You are wealthy. You must be associated with the South Vietnamese government somehow." The truth was just the opposite. Following the takeover, the only wealthy people in Vietnam were those affiliated with the communist government. My parents were surprised the Viet Cong did not execute my great uncle, Tran Van Khac, as they did with many wealthy citizens.

While my great uncle and his two daughters were kept in the concentration camp, my father had befriended the local Viet Cong police department to protect us from any harm. They had asked him--and he offered--to do numerous electrical services for them. They even had invited my family over for dinners, and my parents had them to our house for dinners. According to my older siblings, my father was well respected by the local Viet Cong police and by our neighbors. However, our neighbors thought we were associated with the Viet Cong, so they were afraid of us at the time. Under their covers at night, they were probably whispering to their spouses, "I hope the Viet Cong will not harm us." Any slightest outbursts against the Viet Cong would cost them their lives. (I believe most protesters in a communist country would not live to share their experiences. We are blessed to be living in a free country.)

My father was gifted with excellent communication and leadership skills. (One of my mother's relatives, Chu Thom, once told me, "None of your brothers, not even one, was as smart as your father. I have worked with your father. I know how smart he was.") Due to my father's good relationship with the local Viet Cong police, my great uncle and his two daughters were released earlier than most--after only two years.

According to my oldest brother, Anh Thong, my father was playing a game of chess with a local police friend in 1978. Apparently, authorities had asked if my father had worked for "The Americans." His police friend said, "Two Viet Cong government officials came to our office to ask us if we knew who you were. We told them that you were our friend for years...that you have been the owner of this electronic shop for years...you were not associated with 'The Americans.' We told them that they must have the wrong information about you." My father agreed with his local police friend.

My father knew then that he was under investigation by the Viet Cong government. He had kept a low profile to keep his family safe. Actually, from 1960 to 1969, he did serve for the Americans. His service for the Americans ended six years before the Viet Cong seized control of Vietnam in 1975, so he did not think they would locate that information. As a matter of fact, his former boss had a helicopter assigned for us to leave Vietnam during the last days of 1975, but my father declined the offer. As I mentioned earlier, my aunt (Co Nam) and uncle (Chu Mai), had also tried to persuade my parents to leave, but they had turned down that offer as well.

Prior to the Viet Cong takeover, while my mother was at home managing their retail shop, my father was working for the Americans. In those nine years, he wore multiple hats. His jobs ranged from helping the Navy SEALs, to sending messages to the Viet Cong. My father, among others, would drop paper messages and single band radios from helicopters, encouraging the Viet Cong to stop fighting and come home. He had to be relocated many times and always kept a low profile.

In 1969, while my father was in service at Long An, his mother fell victim to the recklessness of two South Vietnamese soldiers in Da Lat who came into her snack bar and got drunk. While the soldiers were eating and drinking, they took out a grenade, daring each other to pull the pin out and put it back in before it exploded. Being concerned, my father's mother asked her daughter, Co Cuc (my father's half sister), to go outside. Less than a minute later, Co Cuc heard an explosion and ran back inside to find her mother's lifeless body. She was alone and weeping next to her mother's body until she found the strength to move on. Co Cuc then ran a mile to her aunt's house to get help. My father was later contacted but could not come back soon enough for his mother's funeral. He did come later to get his half sister. At the age of 12, she became an orphan. Due to a medical condition, her father had passed away when she was just 9, so after her mother's death, Co Cuc became a part of our family.

Six months later, my father's service for the Americans ended, so he ran for local office (South Vietnamese Government)--and won by only one vote. He then served as a local official for two years and resigned. According to my mother, politics did not make much business sense to my father, so he decided to focus on their business. After he resigned in 1971, my parents sold the business-front house in Long An and moved to Saigon where they built their three-story, business-front house, the one with an electronic repair shop with books to rent.

Chapter 5

The Escape

After my father's chess game with his local police friend, the escape planning and implementation process immediately took place. My father quickly conversed with my great uncle, "The Viet Cong must have found my past records, and I believe I am under investigation." My great uncle replied, "We need to leave. I will help you fund our escape. You take care of the details."

After the Viet Cong took over, they changed the dong currency a few times so that if you hid the cash at home, it would not have any value. In other words, your hidden money became just pieces of paper--worthless. Therefore, my great uncle hid as much gold as he could. Some was hidden beneath his hard floor and some was buried under the ground. A portion of this gold was used to fund our escape.

According to my oldest brother, Anh Thong, my father quickly worked with two friends to plan our escape, and they added two additional families to help fund it. In total, there were to be six families on the boat. The plan was to buy a used fishing boat. If a new boat was built or purchased, the authorities would question it, so a used boat was bought instead. A fishing boat's engine is not strong enough to travel long distances, so a mechanic was brought in to help upgrade the boat with a larger, more powerful engine. Our mechanic was paid very well to keep his silence about our escape. He could not bring in a whole, new larger engine without any suspicion, so he had to dissemble the bigger engine and bring it in by parts and pieces. Then, my father and other men had to help him reassemble it. What should have taken only a month of work, took nearly six months to complete.

    As part of the plan, once the fishing boat was completed, my father applied to work for a company which made depth measurements of the Hau River, a branch of the Mekong River in Can Tho, Vietnam. He was accepted for the job. (Back then, depth measurements were needed to build new routes to transport goods on the Hau River.) As arranged, my father and brother, Anh Minh, worked on this river so the security guards would see them on a daily basis--and become familiar with them as uniformed workers performing jobs on the river. They worked and lived on that boat for three months.

According to my brother, Anh Minh (just a teenager at the time), it was exciting and adventurous. He had a chance to do something different and lived in a completely disparate environment. My brother and father dressed like the locals, socialized and went out to eat local foods which were tasty and unique.

While Anh Minh and my father were working on the boat in Can Tho, my oldest brother, Anh Thong, was helping my mom in Saigon with the electronic repair shop. Each day after school, he worked on his homework and stayed up until midnight to work on the units in the shop. (Astonishingly enough, my oldest brother managed to graduate high school in the top five percent of his class.) Since our nanny and cook were gone, my sister, Chi Dung, had to help with cooking and household chores when she got home from school. (Like my mother, they were--and still are--the walking, talking definition of sacrifice and unselfishness. I am blessed to have such a family. They taught me more by actions than words.) Due to my parents' busy schedules, they had decided to keep my younger brother and me at home. We did not get to go to school.

After staging on the Hau River for three months, my father felt it was safe enough to make the final move. As planned, one afternoon in October 1978, my father and brother first moved out to pick up passengers who were dressed like workers. Then they gathered the rest of the passengers (including me, my mother, my siblings, my great uncle and his two daughters) at different locations in the evening. But when they came to pick up the final passengers, there were twenty extra people who were not originally included in our plan! There were supposed to be only about thirty-two people on the boat, including children, but we ended up with over fifty.

We all promised we would not bring anyone else, but one of the families broke its promise and brought more people. Since everyone had to contribute, this particular family secretly collected additional money from the uninvited group of people. What were we supposed to do with these additional people? Throw them overboard? We had to move forward with them on board, too. (Months earlier, Co Cuc (my father's half sister), her husband and children came over, begging my parents to take them. But my parents honored the agreement. After all, it was a small boat. They sadly said to her, "We are so sorry, but the boat might capsize if too many are onboard.")

Those who were dressed like workers remained on the main deck, and the rest of us were stuffed down inside the two by two feet hole that dropped into the bottom portion of the boat.

The total cost for our escape operation from planning to implementation was about 80 ounces of gold--equivalent to only $24,000 dollars at the time. My great uncle, Tran Van Khac, contributed over 60% of the total cost. Obviously, this escape would not have been possible without my great uncle's offering.

As part of the plan, we also paid a local fisherman to lead us out to sea. Most rivers will eventually empty into a lake, ocean or other body of water. In this case, the Hau River diverged into the Pacific Ocean. At the mouth of the river, where the water slowed and spread out to the sea, some branches were not deep enough for a fishing boat to pass through. If we went on a shallow path, our boat would get stuck, but any fisherman in Can Tho would know the best route to the ocean. Once he got us there, our fisherman turned around… and as the sun was setting, we began to embark on our adventurous journey. A cool breeze was blowing south, which was where we needed to go.

I do not remember being carried into the bottom of the boat, but I do remember my sister waking me up with a "Shhh. We are on our way to America…the land of the free, with great opportunities for our family." At the age of seven, I felt a mixture of excitement and fear all at once. I did not know why or where we were going. We were always taught to respectfully follow directions from our parents and older siblings. Questions were not permitted.

Our goal was to travel south to arrive at the Singapore Refugee Camp, but there were many risks and obstacles ahead of us.

What were these risks and challenges?

1. The uncertain weather conditions on the Pacific Ocean the week of our planned escape.

2. The possibility of becoming lost on the Pacific Ocean.

3. The threat of pirate ships from Thailand that would attack refugee boats for money, gold and other goods. (Refugees brought U.S. dollars and gold with them to exchange for goods and services in order to survive at the Refugee Camp while they waited for the sponsorship process to be completed, which could take over a year. Gold and U.S. currencies were used as a universal form of exchange for goods and services. After the Communists took control, the Vietnamese currency (dong) had very little value outside of Vietnam.)

   When the Thai pirates attacked the refugee boats, they usually took the teenage girls and sold them to the prostitution ring in Thailand. There were opportunities for these pirates to make a great deal of money, and the refugee boats were one of their main targets.

4. The sponsorship process could take over a year, which meant we had to prepare to stay

at the refugee camp for many, many months before we could get a flight to America.

5. Lastly, the risk of getting caught by the Vietnamese Communist authorities--we would all go to jail, or worse.

As planned, we left during the hurricane season (in October) so the Vietnamese coast guards were not available to stop our boat, but we had to face the risk of bad weather conditions at sea. Using a compass and a world map, my father and other men sailed the boat, taking turns so everyone would get some rest.

Chapter 6

On The Pacific Ocean

The weather was nice and cool the night we slipped out to sea. With the exception of the boat's engine running, not a noise was heard. I slept very well on that quiet, first night.

On the first morning, everyone came up from the stuffed bottom to the main deck. My parents gathered our family together and prayed for a safe journey to America. A couple of hours later, I began to feel very sick and so did my younger brother, Man. We felt extreme nausea. What I remembered and thought happened was different from what actually transpired. I remember seeing a hole below our boat. My mother held my brother and I very close to it while we were all seated on the floor. I could see the seawater swaying back and forth, and I was afraid we would fall into that hole. My mother locked one arm around me and the other around my younger brother. While she held each of us in her arms, she asked us to vomit into her hands. I would vomit into her right hand, and she would drop it into the hole. My younger brother would vomit into her left hand and, she would drop it into the hole. We continued to vomit into her hands as she secured us in her arms. But what to me seemed to be a hole on the bottom of the boat was actually an open window in the cabin. I was sick and disoriented so what I "saw" did not actually take place. If there was a hole in the boat, we would have sunk into the ocean.

This act of unconditional love my mother showed us was priceless. Our actions and body language could speak so much louder than any words could convey. (I am not sure if I would have had enough strength to hold my son and daughter in such a fashion, let alone disposed of their vomit in that manner).

As part of the plan, a few necessary items were needed. U.S. dollars, gold, diamonds, and jewelry were packed to be exchanged for goods and services when we arrived at our destination, a refugee camp. Before our journey, some gold was exchanged for U.S. dollars. (The U.S. dollars were--and still are--widely used all over the world. The Vietnamese dong did not have much value because the Viet Cong changed the dong currency several times.) Another necessary item was clothes, but due to the limited space, each person could have only one extra set of clothing. Of course, many foods also had to be brought.

Some of the foods carried on board were dried and dehydrated in order to be kept longer. (When meat or other edible items are dehydrated, moisture is removed so that bacteria, yeast and mold cannot grow. Thus, the dried food will last longer.) My mother and other women brought bags of French baguettes and Banh Mi. Banh Mi is a Vietnamese sandwich, which includes a variety of meat choices inside a French baguette. (The French baguettes or breads were introduced to Vietnam during the French colonial periods.) We also brought Com Nam, which is rice that has been pressed (airtight) and usually flattened into an oval shape to stay fresh longer.

Other cooked and dried meats, such as Thet Cha Bong (known as pork cotton meat) and Thet Kho Tau, were brought to be eaten with Com Nam and French baguettes. Thet Cha Bong was cooked and stirred for hours, so there would not be any moisture left. It can last for a week without refrigeration and will last for months in a refrigerator.

Thet Kho Tau is a dish with marinated pork and boiled eggs in coconut juice. Containers were brought mainly because it was very common, but it does not last longer than a day without refrigeration. Most had to be thrown overboard.

There were also many fresh tropical fruits on board, including coconuts, rambutans, longan, star apples, sugar apples, mangos, oranges, grape fruit, etc. These were some of my favorite fruits, but I was too sick to enjoy most of them.

There were over 50 people on the boat (approximately 34 adults, 12 teenagers and 6 children). The majority were men (about 25 men and only 9 women). Some of the men came uninvited during our passenger pickup.

According to my oldest brother, Anh Thong, the seas were quite rough. The waves were about 15 to 20 feet high, and it felt like our boat was going up and down hills. When seawater got into the boat, the men were very helpful in getting rid of it. Using half coconut shells, they did a good job keeping the seawater out of the boat.

The wind was somewhat strong and the waves were high, so everyone was concerned but remained peaceful. No one was fighting. Some were sick but most were well and relatively calm. Some of the men said, "We should have waited 'till after the hurricane season to leave. We might run into a bad storm and capsize." My father and other men assured them, "The wind is not strong enough. Furthermore, the wind is blowing in the direction we need to go--south. It will help us get to our destination faster." Everyone felt better, but there was still fear and uncertainty all around. The escape was well planned and implemented, but there were many things that were outside of our control.

As the sun was setting on our second night, my father gathered our family to pray again for a safe journey. Our family was mainly in the cabin. My parents were the only ones praying. The others were either atheists or Buddhists. Most Vietnamese claimed to be Buddhists but seldom practice it. (Some see Buddhism as a religion and others as a philosophy.) As evening neared, I felt better and slept well that night.

The sun was rising as our second morning came. I woke up feeling better but still a bit dizzy. I was thirsty and asked my mother for some water, but it tasted as if it was contaminated with oil and gasoline. The water was fine the day before, but some of the men must have handled the oil and gasoline for our boat and did not wash their hands before scooping out some drinking water. My younger brother and I felt sick after we drank some of it, so my mother gave us some fresh tropical fruits and it helped. In the afternoon, we felt better and were able to eat some Com Nam and French baguettes with Thet Cha Bong. It was a delicious meal. Some of the Thet Kho Tau was bad and had to be thrown overboard.

As our boat was sailing south that afternoon, some of the men were able to see dark clouds far behind us. They were yelling to my father and other men, "A storm is coming behind us. We need to sail as fast as possible." The wind started to pick up some more, but it was a cool breeze so heat was not an issue for us. My father and other men were taking turns to sail as fast as they could. The waves got higher; they were about 20 to 25 feet high, which was about 5 to 10 feet higher than the day before. It felt like our boat was going up and down huge slopes. My younger brother and I got sick again. We took turns throwing up until there was nothing left in our stomachs. Also, more seawater was getting in our boat. At times, the men--with their half coconut shells--had to work very hard to get the water out.

As our third night came, the men decided to take turns to monitor our situation. Some men stayed up all night to get water off the boat as needed, while others were assigned to monitor conditions during the day. I did not sleep well that night, so it was harder to get up the next day.

On the next day, I was thirsty again but did not want to drink the contaminated water, so my mother gave me more fresh fruits. I did not want to eat anything, but my mother tried to stuff some food into my mouth, "Please eat, my precious child, so your body can be nourished back to good health."

The wind was blowing even stronger than the day before, and the men were working harder to get the seawater off our boat. Our boat felt like it was going much faster and the waves got even higher (now 20-30 feet high) than the day before. The fierce wind was pushing our boat along, up and down the hilly water--and toward our destination. At this point, our engine was not the driving force anymore. The wind was pushing our boat faster than the engine was capable of doing.

Just when I thought we were going to die, some of the men started yelling, "We can see land! We found land!" In that instant, I felt better. We were all thrilled to see a coastline. But it was Malaysia--not Singapore, which had been our original destination. But we did not care. We were overjoyed and relieved to see land again.

Four hours later that evening, the storm that was chasing us came, knocking down some coconut trees along the beach. But the timing could not have been better; we were safe in a temporary shelter provided by the Malaysian government. A couple of days later, they shipped us to Pulau Bidong Island where we and some Vietnamese refugees stayed until the sponsorship process was completed.

It took us three nights and three days on the Pacific Ocean. This was a very short trip compared to most Vietnamese escapees, whose journeys were typically a week or longer. Other than the difficult weather conditions, our journey was a fairly smooth one. The powerful storm never caught up to our boat, and because we left during the hurricane season, we did not encounter any Thai pirate ships, so we were spared of any robberies, kidnappings or worse. I believe God's hand was at work throughout our risky journey, using a storm to push our boat toward the direction we needed to go! I believe He was answering my parents' prayers.

Chapter 7

Malaysia and Pulau Bidong Island

Even though our voyage was very short compared to most Vietnamese refugees, after three days and three nights on the ocean--with contaminated water, inadequate food, and little shelter--we looked frightening. Furthermore, our clothes were wet and dirty, our skins were sunburned and some of us were sea sick. (With a wet wash cloth, my mother did a good job wiping my younger brother and me.)

When our boat arrived, we got out one-by-one onto the white sand beach of Kuala Terengganu. The local Malaysians ran over and surrounded us. They stared at us as if we were strange-looking sea creatures which had risen from the ocean. In those initial minutes, we felt subhuman and intimidated as the locals peered at us. We had left a lovely home worth 4.2 million dong and were now looked upon as sea rats. It was the most dehumanizing moment of our lives. In any event, we were thankful to be saved. Eventually, Malaysian officers came and took us to a temporary shelter near the beach front.

My parents filled out some paperwork to identify us. My mother brought all of our birth certificates from Vietnam. (Amazingly enough, she still has them today.) Some of the passengers lost their papers or did not bring them so they just tried to identify themselves without any documentation. (Looking back, this could have been a security issue for the rescuing nations. After all, there were about 20 individuals who were not supposed to be on our boat.)

There were two temporary shelters without walls built for refugees. While we were there, hundreds of locals came to see us. They did not come to help, but instead they came to observe us. It was curiosity. At times, we felt like animals at the zoo.

The first night at the temporary shelter, we all slept on the floor using the blankets provided. Some used their handbags as pillows to protect their belongings. The next morning my family and other refugees walked to the markets nearby. My mother stored most of our money and jewelry in her hidden, custom-made pockets, while others carried handbags. Some of us bought a few food items from the market.

The second night, my great uncle's daughter, Bac Thu, strapped her handbag around her shoulder and rested her head on the bag to secure her belongings. As we were asleep, my parents and others heard a loud scream and woke to see a tall, dark male figure running away. The scream came from Bac Thu. She was asleep when the robber violently pulled the handbag from her head, causing the strap to squeeze against her throat, almost strangling her. He quickly ran away with it. We were thankful she was not harmed, but she had lost some money, diamonds and jewelry brought to exchange for goods needed to stay alive. We survived a stormy, dangerous journey and arrived seeking help, only to be robbed by a local. It was discouraging, but we had to move on.

A couple of days later, they shipped us to tiny and uninhibited Pulau Bidong Island. There, they left us to explore and find shelters--but only on the south side. The rest of the island was prohibited, and we were not allowed to cross into other areas. We were one of the first groups of refugees to arrive at Pulau Bidong Island, as it was officially opened as a refugee camp in August 1978, just two months before we arrived. Loud speakers were placed in the surrounding areas so announcements could be heard from the immigration office based on the island.

There was a small building on the island for American immigration officials to handle our correspondence, the sponsorship process and the distribution of donated food items. There were two shifts, one during the day and one at night. It was a 24-hour operation. According to my mother, they did an excellent job processing our letters and documents.

She quickly wrote and sent letters to her siblings, our potential sponsors, in Houston, Texas. As a sponsor, the individual would have to be able to provide food, shelter and clothing until the immigrants were self-sufficient. One of my uncles, Cau Bich, was the best candidate to sponsor us because he was an equipped bachelor at the time. He immediately filled out the necessary paperwork to start the sponsorship process. But even with a sponsor, we were told it could take at least six months to over a year before we could leave the island. As for those who did not have relatives anywhere to sponsor them, they would never forget those warm-hearted individual families, churches, service organizations and private organizations (mainly in the U.S., Canada, France and Australia) that had opened their arms to rescue them.

According to my lovely sister, Chi Dung (then aged 17), Pulau Bidong Island was breathtaking. (Still today, she claims to never have seen such a beautiful beach.) The sand was golden and soft as satin, and the light blue water was crystal clear. Schools of vibrantly colored fish were easily seen in the water. The beach was very clean and surrounded by gorgeous coconut trees. Deeper into the island was a captivating waterfall which flowed into a small pool with large rocks. My sister and others often bathed in that beautiful natural pool. To her, it was like a small tropical paradise without any shelters. It was a vacation island for a seven year-old as well. I did not remember the beauty of the island, but had delightful times floating, relaxing and playing in the seawater.

My parents had brought $6,000 (60 one hundred dollar bills) and four ounces of gold.

Because gold is much heavier, it made better sense to bring more dollar bills than gold. Money and gold were easily stolen, but since my mother was a seamstress, she had made multiple hidden pockets to store the 60 sheets of one hundred dollar bills. This money was intended to be used for emergency expenses.

    According to my oldest brother, Anh Thong, there were about 300 refugees on Pulau Bidong Island, but since we were among the first wave of refugees to arrive there, we had to build our own home. Furthermore, water, food and clothing were scarce at the beginning, so items such as salt, sugar, rice, cans of sardines, dried fish and mung beans were passed out once or twice a week. These were primarily from aid organizations, such as the Malaysian Red Crescent Society and the United Nations High Commissioner for Refugees. Even though it was not enough, we were all thankful for any help given. As months passed, more adequate food supplies were given. We received whole chickens, a better supply of water, and cans of soup, vegetables, coconut milk, and meat.

Other items, including cookies, fresh fruits and vegetables, tar sheets, saws, axes, empty rice bags, cooking pans, bowls, plates, matches, fishing poles, strings, needles and nails were brought by boats to the north (prohibited) side of the island by local Malaysians trying to profit from the refugees who had brought money, mainly U.S. dollars.

My father and brothers had to walk over a mile to get on the north side of the island. They were told that these boats (which were prohibited) would be there for only a short period of time during the day. Since these Malaysians were not allowed on the island itself, only the refugees who could swim out to the boats could buy these items. My father, who could not swim, then had to buy these items--at an additional marked-up price!-- from those who could. So, those refugees who could swim were making money from those refugees who could not. For example, a box of cookies that cost only $7 at the Malaysian market was sold to those refugee swimmers for $18. Those swimmers then sold it to us for $30. We were paying over four times what the item was worth! Regardless, my father bought tar sheets, empty rice bags and other items to build our shelter and to make our lives manageable on the island. My brothers helped my father carry his purchases back. They took multiple trips every week to get these items.

    A number of families had bought saws, so my father and brothers borrowed them to cut down some trees. The wood was used to build the structure of our home. Tar sheets were used to make the roof, and rice bags were used for our walls. Water was needed the most. One well was successfully dug by those who came before us, but it was not enough for everyone so my father and brothers searched for another. They dug until they finally found another well.

    Using the fishing poles and nets they bought from the north side of the island, my father and brothers caught many fresh fish for our dinners. (They caught frogs and used frogs' legs as fish bait.) Floating face down on the shallow seawater with their fishing poles, they awaited a bite and rushed to pull up the fish before it could easily retreat back into the coral. Afterward, my mother would use a match and wood that had been cut down to start a fire and grill the fish or make rice soups. My mother and others would also use the donated bags of mung beans to grow sprouts so we could have fresh vegetables as part of our diet.

According to my mother and sister, there were many enjoyable times on the island. Delicious desserts were made from the beans and coconut milk we were given. Before sunset, groups of people would gather together to eat desserts, sing, dance and tell stories.

In our group alone, many stories were shared. We were fortunate to succeed at our first attempt to escape. A few families were scammed. Thousands of dollars were collected from them and when they came to the appointed place to be picked up, they were left waiting in vain. The perpetrators were gone without a trace.

A few families lost their toddlers during the passenger pickup. One family with five young children got on the rowboat with others. When they arrived to their escape boat, a toddler was missing. For other families, some toddlers fell into the sea during the short journey to their escape boat and still others were left off the boat.

We were blessed to spend only three days and nights on the ocean. Some families endured extended hardship at sea. One family spent two weeks and their boat was robbed twice by two separate pirate ships.

There was a popular Vietnamese song writer, Ngo Thuy Mien, who was also on our boat during the escape. He wrote additional songs for the group to sing. He was a good man and warned a parent in our group, "You have a beautiful seventeen-year-old daughter. You should watch her closely. Please make sure you keep her away from the men and teenage boys here."

After just three months, the heat and living conditions at the refugee camp caused this graceful teenage girl to completely lose her memory. She did not know who she was or the language she was speaking. Her actions were very much like a three year-old. She would play and danced like a child again. In the middle of the night, she was seen running out into the ocean. Her family chased after her. They were afraid she might drown. (Most believed she was possessed by an evil spirit, but I believe it was a combination of the living conditions and her stage of development.) Her aunt once cried, "Of all the teenagers in this island, the devil had to pick the most graceful girl." It was unbearable for them at times but her parents continued to pray for her recovery. The family took turns to care for her.

The family asserted that she preferred the cool weather. In Vietnam, even though they did not have air conditioning, they had a nice home with floor and ceiling fans. She had the luxury of bathing with ice cubes in her bathtub, but on the island there was almost nothing--no house, bed, restroom or electricity.

They did not report her illness because they feared she would be taken to a mental institution in Malaysia and would never see her again. It would also delay their sponsorship process, so they kept the situation a secret.

Two weeks later, my great uncle (Tran Van Khac) and his daughters (Bac Thu and Bac Phuong) were sponsored by a private organization in Canada, as the sponsorship process there was much shorter than the U.S. My great uncle sadly said to my parents, "We are sorry we have to leave you. But I am in my sixties. I cannot survive in these conditions much longer." My mother was in tears, as it was a deeply emotional moment for my parents to say good-bye to Tran Van Khac and his two daughters.

Weeks later, we received news that our sponsorship paperwork was completed and a family interview was scheduled. Other families were also scheduled for interviews, including the family with the teenage daughter who had lost her memory. Since she was ill, another teenage girl offered to go in her place so their sponsorship would not be delayed. Eventually, we learned that we had passed the interview process but were told that it could take months before we could depart the island.

During that waiting period, the sick teenage girl's condition did not improve. During the day, the younger sister was responsible for keeping her sister inside their shelter, while their parents took turns at night to monitor her. As time passed, the younger girl completely disrespected her sister and often screamed at her. "No, you can't play with that! Don't break that! Put it down!" Younger sister would take the items from her teenage sister and put them back. Although the teenage girl was ill, she was never violent. As time went by, we could see that the family had lost hope for her recovery.

Six months later, they announced our departure schedules over the loud speakers. We were thrilled and overjoyed. Unfortunately, the family with the sick girl was still dealing with her illness. But within minutes of the announcement, something incredible happened. The teenage girl picked up a bowl and her younger sister shouted, "Put that bowl down. You can't play with that!" The little sister pulled it out of her hand. The teenage girl gave her sister the most powerful slap on the face and spoke fluently in Vietnamese, "How dare you speak to me that way!" A shock wave was felt through the younger girl's tiny brain as she was lost for a few seconds trying to maintain her balance and comprehend what was going on. Then she realized that her sister was back! "Mom, she is back!" It was another miracle on the island. Just when they thought the teenage girl would remain in that state forever, God freed her just in time.

When the lovely teenager "came back," the beautiful island she once knew was completely different. She went outside her little shelter to see a beach filled with thousands of refugees. Poorly made shelters were just inches apart from one another and trash was seen everywhere, even in the beach water. It had become a crowded, dirty island when she regained her normal mental state.

Whether she was possessed by an evil spirit (like most had thought), or some other reasons, we will never know for sure. What we do know is that she was freed. It was a double blessing for her family.

The day following our departure announcement, we were sent to a temporary camp in Kuala Lumpur, the capital of Malaysia, to await a flight to America. There, we had to go through physical examinations. If the teenage girl was still ill, she would have failed her physical and would have been sent to a mental institution--and that family would be sent back to Pulau Bidong Island. But she was freed just minutes after the announcement and one day before the required physical examinations. God answered her parents' prayers just in time for their departure.

Three days later, we were flown from Kuala Lumpur, Malaysia to San Francisco, California. We then took a bus to Los Angeles and waited there 10 hours before being flown to Houston, Texas, where we were reunited with our extended family. After nine long months at a refugee camp, we finally made it to America.

Chapter 8

Challenges in America

We arrived in Houston, Texas in July 1979, without a penny in our pockets. We were happy to be reunited with our extended family members there, but our challenges were not over. Among other difficulties, we were faced with a language barrier and lack of education. My oldest brother, Anh Thong, had graduated high school in Vietnam (in the top 5% of his class), but my sister (Chi Dung) and older brothers (Anh Minh and Anh Thai) lost one year of school because we were at the refugee camp for nine months. My younger brother, Man (then aged 7), lost two important years of school, kindergarten and first grade. I probably took the hardest blow as I (then aged 8) lost three years of school, kindergarten, first and second grade. As mentioned earlier in the story, due to my parents' hardships after the Communists took control, my younger brother and I never went to school at all in Vietnam.

I remember struggling with school and crying myself to sleep at night. Although my father was a store Manager, the income was not enough. My mother and oldest brother (Anh Thong) were working overtime to help pay the bills. My sister (Chi Dung) and brother (Anh Minh) were working part-time, night shifts, while attending high school. My brother (Anh Thai) was in middle school. My father tried to help me by taking me to the library to check out some books, but the books were useless because no one could read to me. My family was struggling with the language barrier and had virtually no spare time, so they could not help me. I was struggling the most in school, but I did find refuge in two universal languages--Math and Art.

With my father and older siblings working, my parents were able to buy a home--after years of staying at my uncle's rental property. Our family of eight was crowded in the new three-bedroom home. Some of us shared rooms and others had to sleep in the living room. We could not afford much, so my brothers learned to fix their cars and repair just about anything around the house. Due to the limited space, my father and older siblings expanded our house to include two additional bedrooms.

I have forgotten many events in my childhood, but I find it difficult to forget the kindness shown by my very first teacher in third grade. I was wearing flip flops to school, and she asked me what size shoe I wore. Of course, I did not understand a word that was coming from her mouth. Then she tried to measure my feet. A couple of days later, she brought me a brand new pair of shoes. Wow, what a walking and talking definition of kindness! There are moments that happen in our lives that we just cannot forget, and that was definitely one of mine.

Due to the language barrier, I had a few embarrassing moments the first year of school. Here is one that stands out. There was a very cute boy in my class who followed me everywhere I went. I could not understand a single word he was saying, but it was obvious he liked me. I was flattered but puzzled, "Why did he pick me?" I am just a typical Asian girl who can't even speak English! There were many pretty American girls in class with their big, beautiful, round eyes and long gorgeous eyelashes. "Why didn't he follow them?" I wondered. He was very nice to me and based on his body language, sometimes I was able to understand what he was trying to say, but most of the time I just nodded in agreement. One day at recess, I was jumping up to pull some leaves from the tree and the boy asked, "Blah…blah…blah…?" Well, at least that was what I heard. I did not respond so he repeated it. As usual, I just nodded in agreement, as I did not understand. As I was looking up at the leaves and getting ready to jump again, I felt two arms wrap around my stomach and pull me off the ground! I screamed, so a Vietnamese girl from another class ran over to find out what had happened. She spoke to him and then said to me, "He asked if you wanted him to pick you up so you could get the leaves." I was relieved and delighted to hear that. It was surely cute and sweet of him, but I was embarrassed.

I also had a few embarrassing moments when I unknowingly went to the boy's restroom, but I quickly walked out. However, those moments were nothing compared to what happened to a friend of mine when she was in high school.

My friend, Ngoc Anh, came to the States when she was a teenager. It was her first week of school, and she was trying to figure out where she needed to go next after the bell rang. But first she needed to use the restroom, so she went straight into the first one she saw. She speedily got to the stalls, but then noticed the different color paint on them. Quickly, she turned around and saw some teenage boys standing at the urinals. She was shocked--and screamed so loud, that the boys turned around. In doing so, their urine sprayed on the walls and onto each other! The boys then joined her in the screaming parade, and they all ran out. She was embarrassed and immediately apologized to each one of them--and made sure it never happened again.

My parents had their challenges as well. After managing a convenience store for many years, my father lost his job, so my parents opened their own mom-and-pop store, which was just a hole-in-the-wall. They borrowed $50,000 from the bank in order to get started. Due to the heavy traffic getting to and from downtown, they thought it was best to stay there, so a room and kitchen were installed. But because of the location, the store did not do well. My parents only made enough to pay the overhead and for the food. As a result, my older siblings had to take on increased financial responsibility and help pay the bills.

During this period, my younger brother and I were alone most of the time. We saw our father twice a week as he dropped off the home-made food my mother had cooked for all of us. As for my mother, we only saw her once a week when my parents came home for a single night over the weekend in order to attend church on Sunday.

Due to the age gap--and my parents' absence--my older siblings had taken the responsibility of parenting their two youngest siblings. (My sister got married and had left. Anh Minh was pursuing his engineering degree at the University of Texas in Austin.) In addition to acting as our parents, Anh Thong and Anh Thai were employed full-time and took any opportunity to work overtime in order to help pay the bills.

My parents were very successful in Vietnam before the communists took control but now felt like complete failures in the States. It was painful for them to have to rely on their children's incomes. But to us, they were not failures at all. In fact, they were our true heroes. We knew they had tried their best, for we had witnessed their struggles and suffering. Without their extraordinary sacrifice and execution, we would not have had a chance of a better life.

Even though we did not have much growing up in the States, food was never an issue for us. There was always home-made food in our refrigerator. My mother often stayed up after midnight to clean up after she cooked some of the most nutritious and delicious dishes. Due to the healthy food my mother prepared, we were all fit and thin. None of us spoke about exercise and losing weight.

No matter the circumstances, my family always tried to support one another. For example, when I was in high school, if I needed any help with Math, I would wait for my oldest brother, Anh Thong, to come home from work. He was very patient, and his math skills were exceptional. He would help me with any "extra credit" calculus or algebra problem. One day, I remember trying to solve an "extra credit" calculus problem. After thirty minutes, I knew I was not going to be able to solve it, even if a Viet Cong was holding a gun to my head. So, I asked him. It must have been over ten years since he was exposed to any calculus from Vietnam. In fact, he didn't even remember how to solve a calculus problem. He asked me, "Can you show me how you would solve a typical calculus problem?" I showed him and within minutes, he was able to solve my "extra credit" problem. Wow, what an amazing mind! I was thankful for his continuous help. Best of all, he was always patient with his younger siblings.

After high school, each one of us was faced with a decision: should we go to college or get a full-time job? (Despite the language barrier, a year of lost education, and night shifts at a convenience store, my sister and brother, Chi Dung and Anh Minh, managed to make excellent grades in high school!) It was sink or swim; the choice was ours. If we decided to go to college, we had to fund it ourselves, as our parents could not afford to pay for it. Two of us (Anh Minh and I) decided to go to college. My oldest brother continued to work full-time and overtime to help pay the bills. My sister went to college but got married and moved out of town with her husband, Anh Thanh. Due to his job relocations, my sister did not get to complete her college education. My oldest brother and my sister later had successful businesses. Anh Thai went to work for a fast-growing computer company. Man also opted to work full-time.

My parents visited New Orleans (1990)

In 1995, my father suffered a serious stroke which prevented him from performing the simplest tasks such as talking, eating, and bathing. We all were concerned it was too much for my mother to handle at home, but she refused to place him in a nursing home as directed by his doctor. My father was enrolled in a nursing home, but when we came to take him, he was downcast. Once there, my mother was able to see his room. There were four beds and one restroom which meant he would have to live with three other patients sharing one restroom. The room was unsanitary. When she walked in the restroom, she was shocked to see urine and feces on the toilet and on the floor. She quickly turned to us and said, "I cannot leave him here. We have to take him home. I will take care of him." A happy grin was seen on my father's face as he heard the good news. Due to my mother's endless nurturing care, my father survived over ten years from a major stroke which paralyzed the left half side of his body. After ten years under my mother's care, my father peacefully passed away just three months before my wedding. I was saddened to miss him on my wedding day but know he is with our Lord in heaven.

At my wedding reception: Anh Thong and his wife (left), Anh Thai seated next to his wife, Chi Dung and her husband standing behind, my sister-in-law, my mother in the center standing next to me, my husband and my sweet mother-in-law, Anh Minh, his wife and daughter seated, my friend and nephew standing and my younger brother, Man, seated to the right. (2006)

Ultimately, America helped us realize our dreams of having our own home, a decent profession, and a good life. Through perseverance and determination, we overcame many obstacles. We are grateful to be living in America. She has helped countless individuals, such as my family, to accomplish their dreams. Without the U.S., my family would be miserably stuck in Communist Vietnam and crowded into a tiny, dilapidated house for the rest of our lives--that is, if we survived at all. We should each feel blessed to be an American. I know I do!

But obviously not all families that left Vietnam have uplifting stories. I will share one of those here.

Years after we arrived in America, my parents sponsored a Vietnamese family from a Philippine refugee camp. Before the Communists took control of Vietnam, their three children were in private schools and made excellent grades. After the takeover, their kids had to go to public school. Regardless, their oldest daughter, Thao, was at the top of her 11th grade class. She was the apple of their eyes. Her goal was to attend medical school when she arrived in America. But that did not happen. After leaving Vietnam, their boat was robbed by a Thai pirate ship, and the teenage girls (including Thao) were raped on the spot and then kidnapped. People were on their knees crying and begging the pirates to not take their girls, but the families were kicked and beaten. Their dreams were shattered before they could reach a refugee camp.

After a week on the Pacific Ocean, their boat landed in the Philippines. While this family was at the refugee camp, the kidnapped girls were again raped and beaten. Thao took her own life. She dived straight into the blue sea and was never seen again. Most believed those savage pirates were fearful that her spirit would come back to haunt them, so they released the other girls. Days later, the girls were dropped off on the Philippine beach and reunited with their families--with the exception of Thao. Her family was devastated.

In the years that followed, this family stayed with us until they were self-sufficient. In fact, Thao's sister, Ngon, was and--still is--a very good friend of mine.

Today, Ngon is a breadwinner and mother of two very talented twin boys. Her brother, Anh Tri, is a retired engineer managing his wife's pharmacy store and father of two wonderful boys. They missed their sister, Thao, greatly but had to move on.

(God's hand was seen at work throughout my parent's journey through life. They had many trials but God always delivered them through the most difficult times. "The righteous person may have many troubles, but the LORD delivers him from them all", Psalm 34;19)

Reflections

After interviewing my mother and older siblings for this book, I was disappointed to learn that I did not know much about the details of our escape. All of these years, I thought my father and older brothers had built the boat from the ground up. Actually, that would have sparked suspicion from the Communists. Instead, they bought a used boat and had it remodeled with a larger engine.

I also thought the reason my mother was not allowed to drive here was because she had a major accident in Vietnam. Although she had a few close calls on the roads there, she did not have any accidents. With the streets filled with bicycles, motorcycles, mopeds and cyclos, it seemed impossible for anyone to stay accident-free driving a manual transmission vehicle, so I am impressed that my mother was able to drive a motorcar in such traffic for over three years. Even today, I am still perplexed by the fact that my mother was never allowed to drive here in the States. My parents risked their lives escaping Vietnam, so how could my mother's driving be more of a risk than that? Was it a trust issue, a control issue or both? I probably will never know the answer to that question.

Some people asked me, "How did your experiences help shape who you are today?"

I don't know if my experiences truly made me a better person, but they did help me see things through a different lens. We don't know what we have until we have lost it or nearly lost it. My experiences helped me learn to respect and appreciate this country. For example, education was not readily available for everyone in Vietnam, but it is here regardless of your background or circumstances. As parents, we should encourage our children to take advantage of the education available to them as a path to better themselves.

Thoughts on Contemporary America

Due to my love and respect for America, I am saddened to see those here who cause trouble and mayhem, and others who unfairly use the system to profit from this country--and then complain about it. Why would my family and millions worldwide flee to America if she was so horrible? America has helped countless people like my family to realize their dreams, so let's teach our children to respect our country, our educators, and our law enforcement officers. We should try to lead our children by our actions, not just by our words. If they are taught good family values and work hard, they can achieve success in this country, no matter the obstacles.

Escaped Communism But Not Death

In the years following the end of the Vietnam War in 1975, hundreds of thousands fled the brutal Communist rule. (Some estimates put the number well over a million.) In fleeing, tens of thousands perished, most by drowning. Other refugees were kidnapped and murdered by pirates, and many were sold into slavery or prostitution.

My parents--putting their trust in God--left Vietnam (taking me and my five siblings) and victoriously arrived in America. My family successfully escaped Communism, but we will not be able to escape Death itself. That day will come. What we choose to believe is up to us; we all have a choice. But the fact reminds--no matter our decision, we will all perish sooner or later. If we believe and put our trust in God, we do not need to fear Death or what follows. What will I have to gain if I believe in God? I will gain many blessings, such as peace and happiness on Earth-- and eventually eternal life after Death.

God is not done with me yet. I believe He has more challenges and miracles for me in the days to come. He will continue to mold and shape me to become a better person each day.

I believe God kept my family alive for a reason--to share our story.

I would like to share the lyrics to one of my favorite songs, which inspires me to write my story.

My Story

By

Big Daddy Weave

If I told you my story
You would hear hope that wouldn't let go
If I told you my story
You would hear love that never gave up
If I told you my story
You would hear life but it wasn't mine
If I should speak then let it be of the grace
That is greater than all my sin
Of when justice was served and where mercy wins
Of the kindness of Jesus that draws me in
To tell you my story is to tell of Him
If I told you my story
You would hear victory over the enemy
If I told you my story
You would hear freedom that was won for me
If I told you my story
You would hear life overcome the grave
If I should speak then let it be
This is my story
This is my song praising
My Savior all the day long

For an American perspective of the Vietnam War, please see the documentary, "The Last Days in Vietnam", directed and produced by Rory Kennedy.

I hope you enjoyed reading this true story of my family's experiences. If so, please consider leaving feedback on amazon.com. It would greatly be appreciated. Thank you!

If you have any questions or comments, you can also send an email to escapingvietnam@gmail.com

My Father's Family Tree

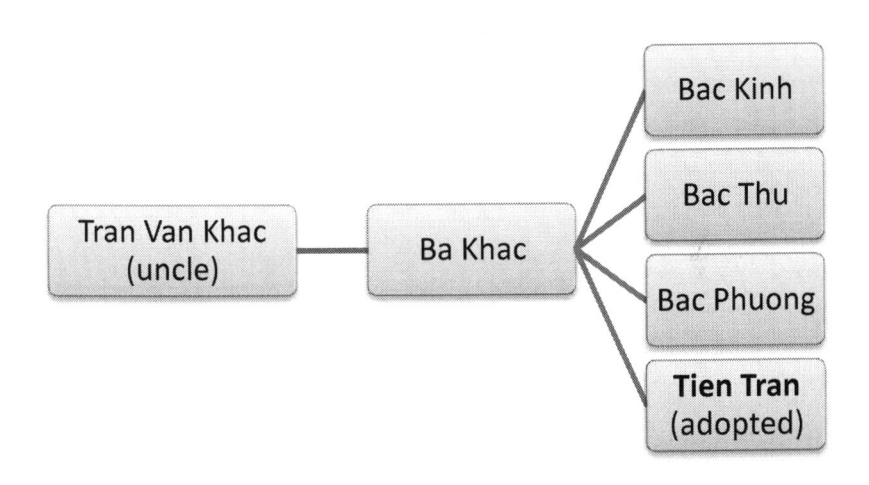

- Tran Van Khac (uncle) — Ba Khac
  - Bac Kinh
  - Bac Thu
  - Bac Phuong
  - **Tien Tran** (adopted)

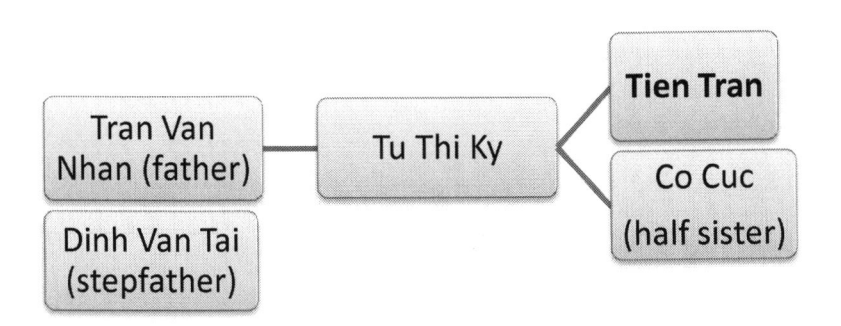

- Tran Van Nhan (father) — Tu Thi Ky
  - **Tien Tran**
  - Co Cuc (half sister)
- Dinh Van Tai (stepfather)

My Mother's Family Tree

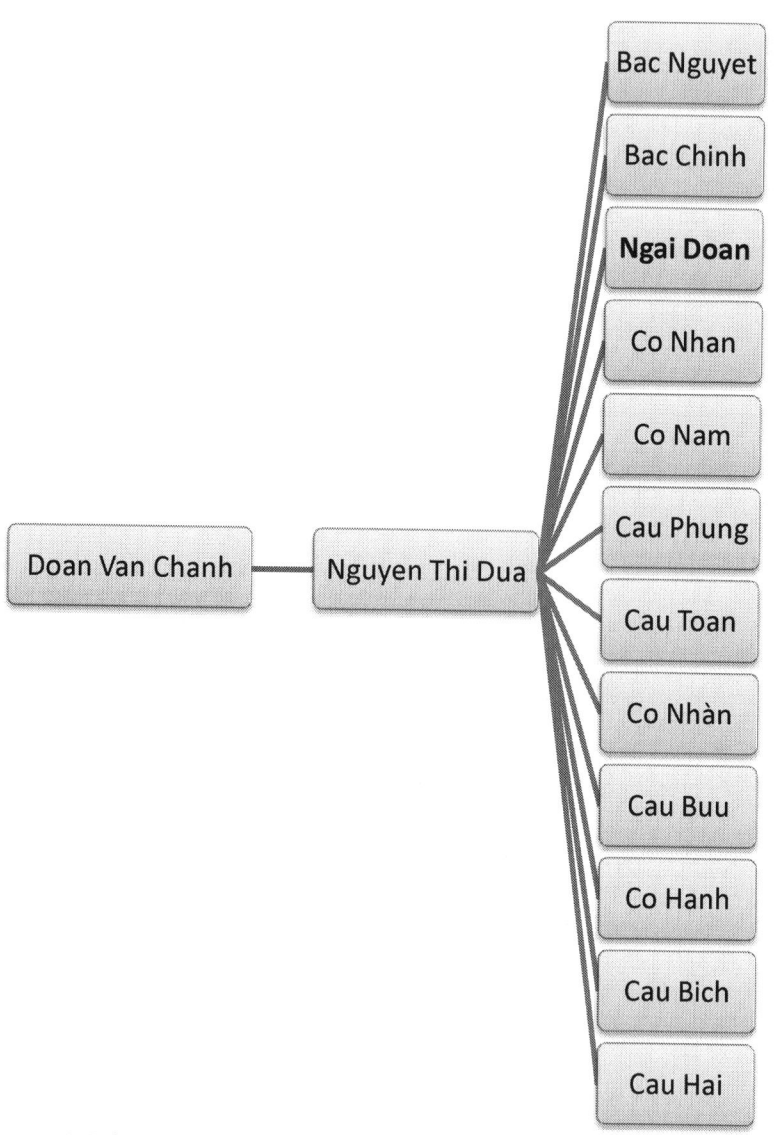

Doan Van Chanh — Nguyen Thi Dua

- Bac Nguyet
- Bac Chinh
- **Ngai Doan**
- Co Nhan
- Co Nam
- Cau Phung
- Cau Toan
- Co Nhàn
- Cau Buu
- Co Hanh
- Cau Bich
- Cau Hai

Bac: A Vietnamese family title for an elder aunt or uncle.
Co: A title for an aunt, a mother's younger sister.
Cau: A title for an uncle, a mother's younger brother.

My Family Tree

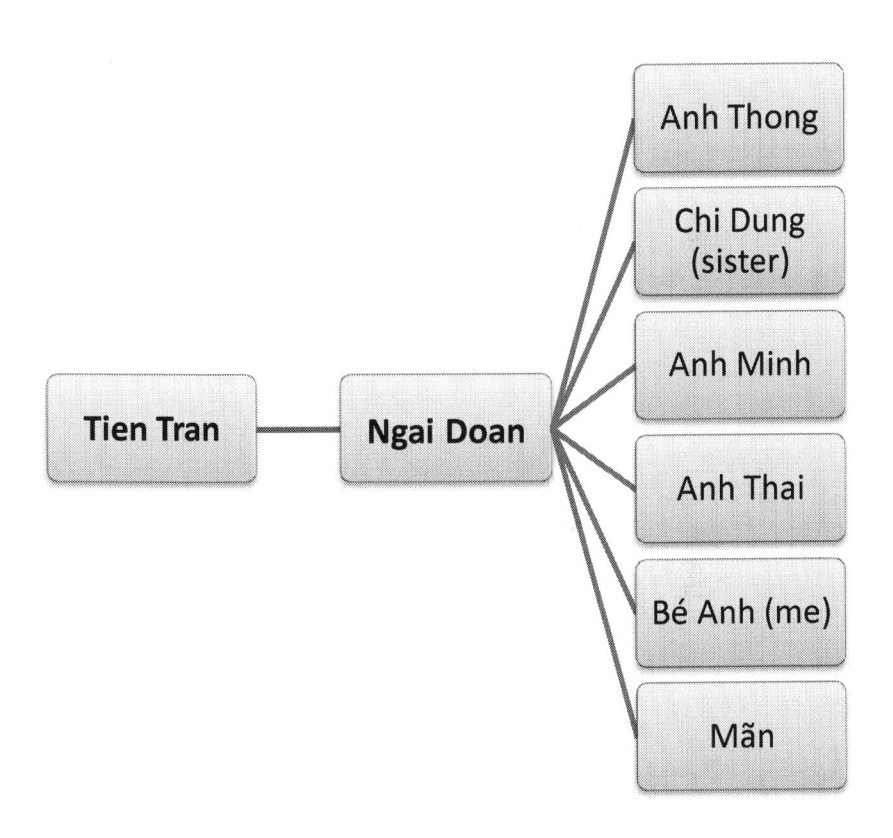

```
Tien Tran ── Ngai Doan ──┬── Anh Thong
                         ├── Chi Dung (sister)
                         ├── Anh Minh
                         ├── Anh Thai
                         ├── Bé Anh (me)
                         └── Mãn
```

Anh: A Vietnamese family title for an older brother.
Chi: A family title for an older sister.
Bé: A family title for a baby sister. To my family, I am stuck with that title.

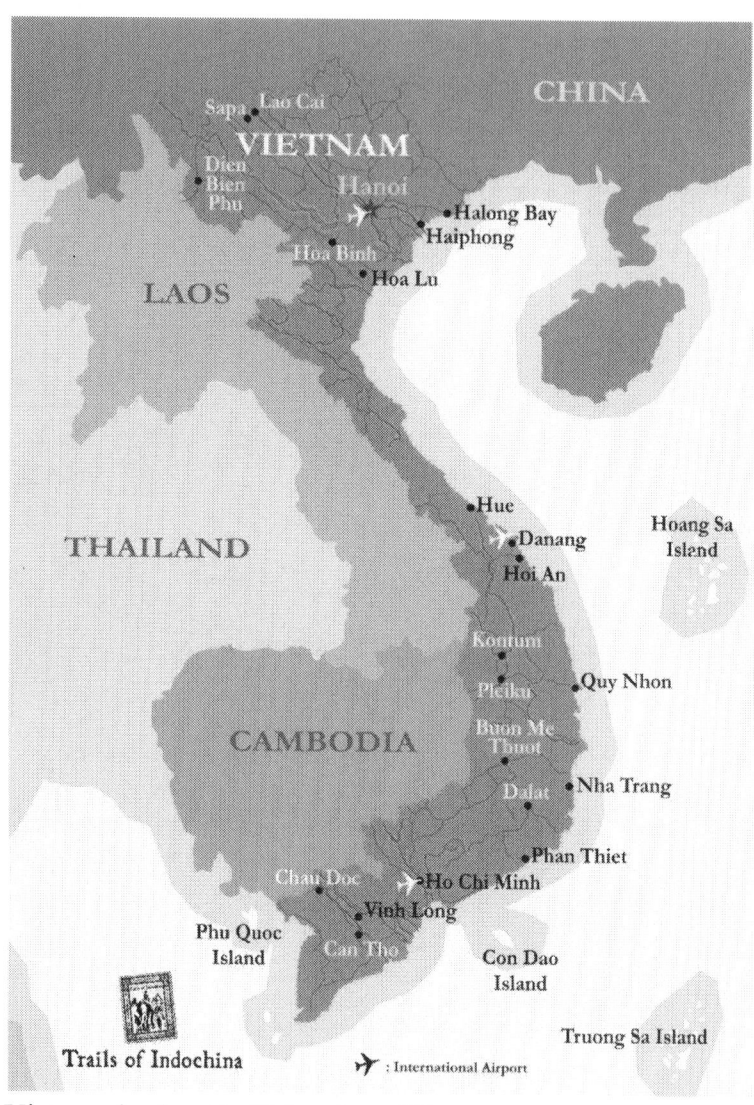

Vietnam is about half the size of Texas.

Glossary

AO DAI: A popular Vietnamese dress with long-sleeves and ankle panels at front and back; worn with long, thin silky pants.

CAN THO: A city known for its floating markets, approximately 105 miles southwest of Ho Chi Minh (Saigon) and located on the south bank of the Hau River.

COMMUNISM: A system of social organization in which all economic and social activities is controlled by a single dominating government.

CYCLO (XICH LO): A three-wheel bike with a one or two-seated carriage, safe to carry passengers for short distances.

DA LAT: or Dalat (one word) A city approximately 186 miles northeast of Saigon. It is famous for its beautiful waterfalls and spring-like weather year-round.

DONG: Vietnamese currency.

HANOI: A city approximately 720 miles north of Saigon and is the capital of Vietnam.

HAU RIVER: A southern branch of the Mekong River in Can Tho that leads to the Pacific Ocean.

HOI CHO: A fall festival which includes food, live bands, beauty and fashion shows, games, arts and crafts.

LONG AN: A province approximately 35 miles from Saigon located within the Mekong Delta region of southern Vietnam.

PLEIKU: A city located in the Central Highlands of Vietnam, approximately 314 miles northeast of Saigon. It is the capital of Gia Lai Province and known to house a strategic South Vietnamese base during the War.

PULAU BIDONG ISLAND: A small uninhabited island, approximately one square mile area, belonging to Malaysia.

QUE: Countryside or rural areas of Vietnam.

SAIGON: A city which became Ho Chi Minh City after the Fall of Saigon in 1975. Ho Chi Minh was named after the first communist leader of North Vietnam.

THU DUC: A district in the northeast of Saigon.

VIET CONG: Vietnamese Communists who originated in North Vietnam.

VUNG TAU: A city approximately 70 miles southeast of Saigon and was known as the crude oil extraction center of Vietnam.

About The Author

Ann Tran-Mace was born in Saigon, Vietnam in 1971. In 1978, three years after the fall of Saigon, she and her family escaped by boat to a refugee camp, and finally settled in America in 1979.

Despite the language barrier and having lost three years of education, she graduated high school and became a U.S. citizen at the age of 18. She later earned a bachelor's degree in Operations Management from the University of Houston.

Today, she resides in Houston, Texas with her husband, Rick, and two children, Matt and Lila.

It was difficult for her to re-live the past and write about it. But, it was all well worth it.

Made in the USA
Lexington, KY
21 September 2018